Automobiles

Anne Fitzpatrick

A+
Smart Apple Media

GREAT INVENTIONS

✎ Published by Smart Apple Media

1980 Lookout Drive, North Mankato, MN 56003

Designed by Rita Marshall

Copyright © 2004 Smart Apple Media. International copyright reserved in all countries. No part of this book may be reproduced in any form without written permission from the publisher.

Printed in the United States of America

✎ Photographs by Artemis Images (ATD Group), Gary J. Benson, Corbis (AFP, Bettmann, Hulton-Deutsch Collection, Lake County Museum), Richard Cummins, Tom Myers, Photo Researchers, Inc. (Georg Gerster)

✎ Library of Congress Cataloging-in-Publication Data

Fitzpatrick, Anne, 1978– Automobiles / by Anne Fitzpatrick.

p. cm. – (Great inventions) Includes bibliographical references.

Summary: An introduction to the ideas and technical developments that produced today's automobiles. Includes a "hands on" activity.

✎ ISBN 1-58340-319-1

1. Automobiles–History–Juvenile literature. [1. Automobiles–History].

I. Title. II. Great inventions (Mankato, Minn.).

TL147.F54 2003   629.222–dc21   2002042794

✎ First Edition 9 8 7 6 5 4 3 2 1

CONTENTS

Automobiles

A Distant Dream	6
Success at Last	12
Good-bye Horses	14
Today and Tomorrow	16
Hands On: Invent an Automobile	22
Additional Information	24

A Distant Dream

More than 500 years ago, a great artist and inventor named Leonardo da Vinci drew the first automobile. But he was born too soon to be able to bring his drawing to life. He knew how it would be driven, but he did not know how to make it go. It would be several hundred years before the first car, called a "horseless carriage," would be built.

When the steam engine was invented in 1712, people tried to use it to make vehicles go. In 1769, a French inventor named

Passengers on a "horseless carriage" in 1897

Nicholas Joseph Cugnot built a three-wheeled truck powered by steam. Cugnot's truck would run for only 15 minutes before it ran out of steam and had to stop and boil more water.

In 1803, an Englishman named Richard Trevithick built a passenger car powered by steam. Trevithick developed his idea into the first railroad locomotive. Soon the countryside was criss-crossed with railroad tracks. But the steam engine was too large and heavy to power a small road vehicle.

The word "automobile" comes from Greek words that mean "moves by itself."

A steam locomotive running along railroad tracks

Early on, only rich people could afford automobiles

The automobile dream would have to wait until the invention of the gas engine.

Success at Last

In 1862, an inventor named Etienne Lenoir drove the first automobile through a forest in France. The automobile was an old horse cart with an engine mounted between the wheels. This **internal-combustion engine** used small explosions to create power. An electric spark lit a mixture of gas and air. The explosions moved **pistons**, which in turn moved a **drive shaft** that turned the wheels. ✎ In 1885, a German inventor

named Carl Benz finished the first automobile sold to the public.

It had three wheels, created as much power as three horses, and could reach a top speed of 20 miles (30 km) per hour.

The famous 1885 automobile made by Carl Benz

Good-bye Horses

People were a little afraid of automobiles at first. Some even disliked them because of the noise and smell they created. But inventors worked hard to improve the automobile. Benz and fellow German Gottfried Daimler, Frenchman Louis Renault, American Charles Duryea, and other people came up with new car designs faster than they could build them. 🖎 One man had a unique vision for the automobile. A young American named Henry Ford wanted

Wheels were invented about 6,000 years ago. The air-filled tires used today were invented in 1845.

to build a car that everyone could afford. He set out to do it by using new ideas about **mass production**. It was much cheaper and faster to build thousands of cars that were exactly

An assembly line at one of Henry Ford's factories

alike, all at the same time, than to build each car individually.

Ford introduced an affordable car called the Model T in 1908.

By 1930, more than 15 million Model Ts had been sold.

Today and Tomorrow

As automobiles became more popular and common, many different kinds were developed. Today there are sports cars, luxury cars, trucks, vans, family cars, and race cars. Networks of streets and highways connect everything, and there are countless gas stations, parking lots, and drive-

North America has thousands of roads and highways

through windows. ✍ The world seems smaller since the invention of the automobile. People can live farther away from each other and move around more. Cars have also made people more independent. When the first automobiles were designed, many were meant to carry a crowd of people. Traveling alone was unthinkable—only kings and very wealthy or important people traveled alone.

The first highway was built in Berlin, Germany. It was called the Autobahn and doubled as a racetrack.

Today, people travel alone all the time. ✍ In the future, automobiles will continue to become faster and more powerful.

They will also become safer. Automobile companies are always trying to find ways to better protect drivers and passengers.

The fuel that cars use is one important safety and practical

Too many cars on the road creates traffic problems

concern. Gasoline pollutes the air when it is burned, and the oil from which it is made will someday run out. Automobiles of the future may use other fuels, such as **ethanol**, solar (sun) power, or electricity. Some cars today called "hybrid" cars use both gasoline and electricity. Only time will tell where the road may take us, but one thing is for sure—the automobile is here to stay!

Some early cars had seats in front of the driver. The driver looked over the passengers' heads to see the road.

This small, odd-looking car is powered by electricity

Invent an Automobile

We have come a long way from the first cars that automobile inventors drove more than 100 years ago. Imagine how different cars will be in another 100 years! In this activity, you can design your own automobile.

What You Need

Magazines
Scissors
Markers or crayons
Construction paper
Glue

What You Do

1. Look through the magazines and find pictures of cars to cut out.
2. Cut out the parts of the cars that you like.
3. Glue the different car parts onto the construction paper, creating your own car.
4. With the markers and crayons, add on whatever parts you want your car to have.

Automobiles come in all colors, shapes, and sizes

Index

Benz, Carl 12-13, 14
car designs 14, 16, 22
Ford, Henry 14-16
fuel 12, 19-20
gas engines, 12
Model T 16
pollution 20
roads 16, 18
steam engines 6, 8

Words to Know

drive shaft (DRYV shaft)—a rod or pole that connects a car's engine to the wheels

ethanol (EH-thuh-nol)—a fuel made from corn that can be used in place of gasoline

internal-combustion engine (in-TER-nul-cum-BUS-chin EN-jin)—a motor inside which an explosion takes place to create power and push a machine forward

mass production (MASS pro-DUK-shin)—building large numbers of one thing at the same time

pistons (PIS-tunz)—solid objects, shaped like soup cans, that move up and down inside an engine to make a car move

Read More

Oxlade, Chris. *Take It Apart: Car*. London: Thameside Press, 2003.

Platt, Richard. *Smithsonian Visual Timeline of Inventions*. London: Dorling Kindersley, 1994.

Sutton, Richard. *Eyewitness Books: Car*. New York: Alfred A. Knopf, 1990.

Internet Sites

BrainPOP: Cars
http://www.brainpop.com/tech/transportation/cars/index.weml

Early Adventures with the Automobile
http://www.ibiscom.com/auto.htm

The Henry Ford Museum
http://www.hfmgv.org

Mercedes-Benz for Kids
http://www.mercedes-benz.com/d/about/kids/index.html